PIANO SOLO

Disney
MALEFICENT
MISTRESS OF EVIL

MUSIC FROM THE MOTION PICTURE SOUNDTRACK

T0084063

ISBN 978-1-5400-8187-2

Motion Picture Artwork TM & Copyright © 2019 Disney

HAL•LEONARD®

Visit Hal Leonard Online at
www.halleonard.com

Contact us:
Hal Leonard
7777 West Bluemound Road
Milwaukee, WI 53213
Email: info@halleonard.com

In Europe, contact:
Hal Leonard Europe Limited
42 Wigmore Street
Marylebone, London, W1U 2RN
Email: info@halleonardeurope.com

In Australia, contact:
Hal Leonard Australia Pty. Ltd.
4 Lentara Court
Cheltenham, Victoria, 3192 Australia
Email: info@halleonard.com.au

CONTENTS

MISTRESS OF EVIL

Music by GEOFF ZANELLI

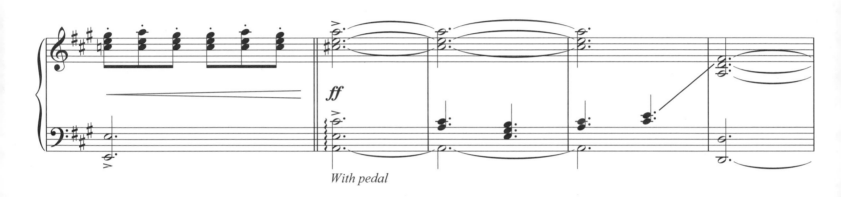

ULSTEAD

Music by GEOFF ZANELLI

Very slowly

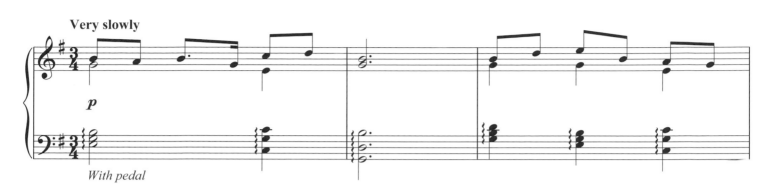

p

With pedal

YOU DON'T HAVE TO CHANGE

Music by GEOFF ZANELLI

HELLO, BEASTIE!

Music by GEOFF ZANELLI

YOU CAN'T STOP THE GIRL

Words and Music by BLETA REXHA,
NATE CYPHERT, MICHAEL POLLACK,
ALEX SCHWARTZ, JOE KHAJADOURIAN,
SEAN NELSON, JEFF J. LIN,
EVAN SULT and AARON HUFFMAN

oh,   but she's so brave, _ though.   Just like a tor - na -

- do,   she's tak - ing us by storm. _____   You can't stop the girl _

____ from go - ing, you can't stop the world __ from know - ing. The truth will set you free, _

(play eighth notes second time)

_____ oh.   You can't stop the girl __

TIME TO COME HOME

Music by GEOFF ZANELLI